100
HOUSES

CATHY STRONGMAN
PHOTOGRAPHY BY **VIEW**

100
HOUSES
MODERN DESIGNS FOR
CONTEMPORARY LIVING

MERRELL
LONDON · NEW YORK

Contents

Introduction

6

If you ask a child to draw a house, the likely result will resemble a brick box with a pitched roof and small, square windows, perhaps adorned with a dash of colour in the form of a bright-red door. This has become the well-established stereotype of the home. But if we were to ask a child in fifty years' time to repeat the exercise, would the drawing be the same? As the 100 houses in this book demonstrate, the conventional notion of what a house should look like is changing rapidly. For example, Crescent House by Make (**1**) abandons the traditional box-like form in favour of two interconnecting crescent-shaped volumes, while Spine House (**2**), the first home by Sir Nicholas Grimshaw, is a glass box with a wooden, cocoon-shaped 'spine' apparently rocketing through its centre.

In the past, architects had to rely for the most part on locally available materials, leading to the evolution of distinct vernacular styles. Today's architects have at their fingertips a multiplicity of diverse materials and construction techniques, providing endless opportunities for radical designs independent of geographical location. The gull-wing-shaped roof of Alan Power's Portobello Road Houses (**3**) would have been inconceivable seventy years ago, as would the zinc-clad Focus House by Bere Architects (**4**, **5**). Modelling software has also developed rapidly, allowing architects to construct three-dimensional models of gravity-defying forms that can be translated into real buildings. The shortage of conventional building sites, especially in crowded urban centres, has also made architects think more imaginatively about how they can squeeze a building on to an irregular plot, anchor a home to a steep hillside or, in many cases, reinvent an existing building.

For every architect-designed home there is a client, and some of the credit for the proliferation of bold contemporary architectural styles must go to the homeowners who have dared to break away from the stereotype. A growing number of owners are no longer willing to settle for uninspiring developer-built homes, which all too often embody a pastiche of previous styles. Most impressive is the willingness of many of these clients to commission homes in which a high priority is given to environmental considerations. The

1

3

2

7

4

5

construction industry as a whole faces an enormous task in its obligation to respond to the 'green' agenda, but it is often only when clients are willing to experiment with unfamiliar materials and install new eco-friendly technologies that architects can create truly innovative buildings. Some of the projects in this book, such as the Dyke Road House by BBM Sustainable Design (**6**) and The Retreat by Buckley Gray Yeoman (**7**), demonstrate how both existing and new-build houses can be adapted in imaginative ways to meet the environmental challenges that lie ahead.

The changing nature of clients' briefs to architects offers an intriguing insight into how our living habits – and what we ask of our living spaces – are evolving. There are numerous examples below of Victorian and Edwardian homes that have been gutted and reconfigured to create free-flowing spaces. In renovated and new houses alike, such relatively formal areas as the dining-room have been abandoned and replaced by more relaxed open-plan kitchen and dining spaces. Flexibility has also become a common requirement, as exemplified in a house by Brady Mallalieu Architects (**8**, **9**), which has moveable walls, while the second bedroom in the holiday home by Tzannes Associates (**10**, **11**) is equipped with a desk that opens up into a double bed. In addition, leisure activities are an increasingly important part of home life. A surprising

number of houses in this book incorporate swimming pools, while others have cinemas and gyms, and one even has a squash court contained within its walls.

Certain architectural trends take hold all over the world. Capturing an abundance of natural light has become the holy grail of domestic architecture; making the best use of any views is another crucial requirement. Many clients ask for their living spaces to extend outdoors, and numerous houses described here have huge retractable glass doors that can be opened to allow the occupants to obliterate the boundary between indoor and outdoor living. One example is a house by Chenchow Little Architects (**12**), where almost every ground-floor wall can be slid open to create a seamless transition from living space to surrounding landscape.

It is tempting to conclude that the ubiquity of these elements – the open-plan living areas, the great façades of glass, the crisp white walls – signals the globalization of the architectural styles first proposed by the early twentieth-century Modern Movement. It is true that the communication of ideas through print media and the Internet and the opportunities for architects to work in many different countries have led to the dissemination of certain key trends across the globe. Yet what is heartening about the houses featured in this book is the sheer variety of forms and aesthetic qualities,

and the way in which they are designed specifically to harmonize with the surrounding landscape, climatic conditions and cultural setting. For example, a house by Wingårdhs (**13**) is clad in untreated cedar so that with age the building will turn silvery grey to merge with its coastal setting. A house by McLean Quinlan is built from stones reclaimed from the farmhouse it replaces (**14**, **15**), and the house by KNTA Architects in Singapore (**16**) has a double-layered roof to protect the interiors from the intense heat of the sun.

These site-specific solutions, coupled with the inventive use of materials and the efforts to create homes that respond to modern patterns of living, ensure that contemporary architecture continues to develop in many different directions. Houses are the most common type of building in the world and they are also the buildings that mean most to humans on a personal level. It is therefore both reassuring and exciting to see so many talented architects designing residential buildings that are often courageous in concept, but also practical and individual.

Skywood

Graham Phillips
Buckingham, Buckinghamshire, UK

The aspiration of architect Graham Phillips of Foster + Partners when designing this house was to create 'a glass box in the woods'. The four-bedroomed family home in Buckingham stands in 0.2 hectares (½ acre) of mature woodland and is carefully positioned to take advantage of views over a lake. It consists of two single-storey rectangular blocks incorporating enormous expanses of glass. Facing east is a bedroom block that doubles as one side of a walled garden. Raised to a slightly higher level and defined by its crisp cantilevered roof is the living block, with a main reception room that offers views down the lake to a small island. The limestone floor of the living area extends through the glass wall to create an exterior terrace. Indoor spaces are artfully designed for flexibility of use. The combined kitchen and dining area incorporates sliding and folding partitions and movable tables; it can be arranged as either an open-plan kitchen/diner or a more formal dining-room with the kitchen hidden from sight. Perfectly in harmony with its setting, this house is the epitome of understated elegance.

House and Studio

Patel Taylor
London, UK

By making sensitive changes and additions to this detached suburban house in Putney, south-west London, the architect Patel Taylor has provided extra living accommodation and brought more natural light into the existing spaces. A glass-roofed extension to the side of the building creates a bright, contemporary kitchen, which has been given an additional glass door leading out on to the newly installed shaded patio. This outdoor entertaining space can also be reached through two further glass doors inserted into the rear façade of the building.

On the other side of the garden from the patio is a separate studio. The main body of this structure consists of a living-room encased in wood and glass and made snug by the addition of a woodburning stove. The glass façade of the building is partly hidden behind a wicker façade, with the space in between filled by a flowerbed and wires supporting climbing plants. Surrounded by lush foliage, the studio provides the occupants with a secluded retreat cut off from the daily hustle and bustle that characterizes their home.

Cliff House

Walters and Cohen/Collins and Turner Architects
Sydney, New South Wales, Australia

Generous expanses of glass allow this compact house, which perches delicately on the 80-metre-high (265 ft) sandstone cliffs of Bondi Beach, to take full advantage of views across the Pacific Ocean. It consists of two rectangular forms, positioned at an angle to each other to create an irregularly shaped double-height entrance hall and stairwell, with an internal courtyard at the far end. Four bedrooms are on the ground floor, and it is only after visitors have ascended the stairs that they can appreciate the full impact of the dramatic panoramas. At this first-floor level, a further bedroom and a more enclosed kitchen and dining-room are incorporated within the rear rectangular form, while a large flowing space with informal areas for sitting, eating and cooking is adorned by full-length windows overlooking the sea. An additional band of glass, on which the roof of the house hovers, introduces more light and enhances the house's impression of weightlessness.

Spine House

Grimshaw

Oberkülheim, Bergisch Gladbach, Germany

4

The Spine House is the first one-off home designed by British architect Sir Nicholas Grimshaw, in collaboration with Mark Bryden and Martin Wood. The building consists of an industrial steel-framed glass box pierced at its centre by a timber 'spine' resembling an aeroplane fuselage. The spine forms the entrance hall and cumulates in a bow-shaped balcony that juts out over the garden. The architects have created a 'house within a house', an organically shaped structure beautifully handcrafted from American ash, providing a womb-like space where the owners can relax and enjoy the rural views. Within the steel-and-glass box, the space is arranged so that the bedrooms, two studies and living, kitchen and dining zones are at the front; their double-height glazed walls open out the house to the surrounding landscape. The rear of the property contains the garages, utility rooms and an internal squash court and swimming pool. This is a bold design that dispenses with convention and yet provides a luxurious and practical retreat.

Bacon Street House

Pentagram Architects
London, UK

5

Bethnal Green in east London has a great variety of buildings, including tatty brick-built shops, steel-clad warehouses and recent developments made mainly from London stock brick. William Russell of Pentagram Architects has added to the district's eclectic mix by building himself a four-storey house that bears little resemblance to a home. Three materials were used to clad the reinforced-concrete frame: Alwitra, a roofing membrane, wraps over the roof and down the rear wall; the ground and first floors are faced in galvanized steel; and the rest is encased in clear- and white-laminate double-glazed units, creating varying degrees of translucency and transparency. Flexibility of use was a key element in the interior layout. The ground floor and basement form a self-contained unit, which could be reconnected with the rest of the house. The first floor has two bedrooms and a bathroom; the second a kitchen and living area; and the third a small study with access to the roof terrace. While double-height spaces are included at basement and second-floor level, there are also more intimate enclaves.

28

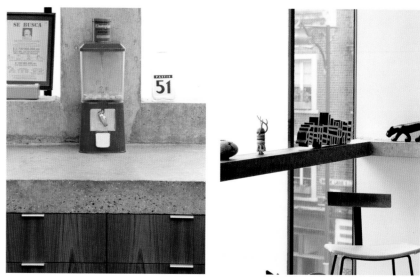

Lotus House

Kengo Kuma & Associates
Kanagawa, Japan

6

This holiday home in Japan slips sympathetically into its woodland setting. The Lotus House stands by a quiet river, deep in the mountains of Kanagawa prefecture. Its two wings are divided by a terrace that connects the woods at the back of the house with those on the opposite side of the river. A pond filled with lotus plants between the house and the river brings the landscape through the house. This effect has been exaggerated by the generous use of glass and the unusual cladding, which consists of travertine stone plates suspended from a delicate

and virtually invisible lattice of steel chains, giving the exterior of the building a porous and translucent quality. One wing accommodates a garage, two bedroom suites and the open-plan kitchen and dining area; a sculptural staircase leads up to a bathroom and sauna. The second wing houses a large living-room. The whole building exudes a sense of tranquility that perfectly matches the serenity of the site.

Refurbished House

PTP Architects
London, UK

7

When the clients bought this house in central London it was divided into a series of poorly connected rooms that were generally poky and dark. PTP Architects has reconfigured the internal layout to create a series of large, naturally lit rooms that flow into one another. The spacious entrance hall leads through double doors to the main reception room, where the ceiling was cut away to create a vast rooflight, and from where full-height glass doors lead to a small terrace. In the basement, the architect excavated an additional 80 centimetres (32 in.) to give more height in what is now an open-plan kitchen, living- and dining-room, and added folding glass doors to the garden. Two bedrooms occupy the first floor. The master bedroom has an en suite bathroom with a rooflight, while a bathroom for the second bedroom slots into a newly built attic extension with an entirely glazed roof. Lavish materials, including dark American walnut joinery, Crema Marfil stone and even a cashmere headboard in the master bedroom, complete the opulent look of the reconfigured spaces.

Smith House

Randles Hill Straatveit

Beauty Point, New South Wales, Australia

8

Randles Hill Straatveit (now Randles Straatveit Architects) has given this 1930s bungalow in Beauty Point, New South Wales, a modern makeover. The client required more room and a better flow of spaces than the segregated rooms provided. Not only was the house expanded with various additional structures, but also it was provided with a new entrance, staircase, living spaces, kitchen, bedrooms and bathrooms. The internal spaces were reorganized to create an improved circulation route through the building, while formal and private zones are now better defined. Built-in storage makes better use of the space. The focus is now the breakfast room, which was slotted in at landing level. Timber joinery, bright white walls and rooflights combine to enhance the contemporary feel, and large panes of glass reconnect the house to its surrounding lush landscape.

Butterfly House

9

Chetwoods Architects
Dunsfold, Surrey, UK

This extraordinary building incorporates every stage of the butterfly's development, from the larva, represented by the walkway, to the chrysalis, captured by the staircase and conservatory, to the emergence of the insect, as seen in the enormous winged canopies that project from the rear of the building. The refurbished house, which took three years to evolve, encompasses an unorthodox selection of materials, including more than 100 metres (330 ft) of fibre optics, nearly 50 interwoven carbon-fibre fishing rods for the handrails, 2 kilometres (1¼ miles) of bungee rope to construct the seating area and exterior pergola, and 200 metres (660 ft) of irrigation tubing for the walkways and pergola structure at the front. As well as offering a dramatic and unique experience, the building is also a comfortable family home. Furthermore, more than two hundred lavender, hebe and buddleia plants have been used to attract butterflies to this singular residence, which draws so heavily on their life cycle for its inspiration.

Nicklin House

Levitate Architecture and Design Studio
London, UK

10

The ground floor of this Edwardian house in Wimbledon, south-west London, has been transformed. Formerly, the kitchen and living-room were sandwiched between two reception rooms at the front and a lean-to conservatory and dining-room at the rear. The architect stripped away the rear additions and replaced them with a new single volume containing an open-plan living, dining and kitchen area. Full-height sliding glass doors link these spaces with the south-east-facing garden, while a rooflight running the width of the extension admits additional natural light. This feature is made even more exciting by the bi-axial etched-glass canopy (with vertical and horizontal slats), which animates the interior with constantly changing patterns of light and shadow. A matching canopy shades the terrace. Running along the back of the living area are a storage room and a bathroom, while the kitchen has doors on to the playroom at the front of the house. The new layout creates a free-flowing series of spaces, all of which now enjoy natural light and views on to the street or the garden.

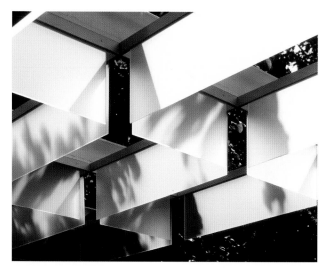

Tower House

Atelier Bow-Wow

Tokyo, Japan

11

Tower House occupies a very narrow strip of land in the Shinagawa-ku district of Tokyo. Designed by Atelier Bow-Wow, the fortress-like home, constructed from reinforced concrete, measures a mere 3 × 6 metres (10 × 20 ft) and is 11.5 metres (38 ft) high. A large expanse of living space fits ingeniously into a confined shell. Doing away with the traditional, space-consuming enclosed stairwell and internal partition walls, the design comprises a series of nine rooms, arranged on staggered levels around a staircase suspended in a central void. The open treads of the staircase float between steel supports that physically separate the rooms while allowing people in different parts of the house to see and talk to one another. It is both a flowing single space and a series of defined areas that feel light and spacious rather than oppressively small. By abandoning the conventional wisdom about how a house should be arranged, the architect has demonstrated that even the most awkward of plots can be transformed into a practical and exciting contemporary home.

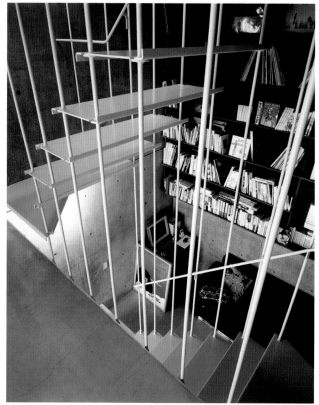

Collage House

Jonathan Tuckey
London, UK

12

Occupying a former industrial site in Kilburn, north London, Collage House is a brilliant conversion from a jumble of old buildings centred on a steel workshop. Jonathan Tuckey's challenge was to create a family home while retaining the site's gritty character. A narrow, box-shaped entrance is the only part of the building visible from the street. The house has three elements: the entrance hall and living area with a mezzanine study leading to a guest bedroom and bathroom above; the kitchen and dining-room, which occupy the former workshop area; and

a new two-storey structure, which holds the main bedrooms and a bathroom. The outermost buildings were demolished to create a garden courtyard, enclosed by the bedroom wing. Original features, such as the workshop's bowstring truss roof and the ink-splattered brick walls, were left exposed and are complemented by modern utilitarian materials, such as the black concrete floor, enamelled work surfaces and garden taps in the kitchen, the exposed Douglas fir studwork walls throughout, and the exterior cladding of larch plywood panels.

Dyke Road House

13

BBM Sustainable Design
Hove, East Sussex, UK

Formerly a nondescript 1950s building incorporating a pitched roof and a coat of hanging tiles, this house, on the south coast of England, was radically upgraded to produce a home that combines a host of environmentally friendly elements with a stylishly modern appearance. The skeleton of the building is intact but, by extending its footprint into the garden, and by gutting and redesigning the ground floor, the architect created a large open-plan living, dining and kitchen area. A studio was built above the flat-roofed garage, while the attic was extended upwards to provide an additional bedroom. Sustainable materials were used wherever possible, including jute and recycled-newspaper insulation, clay plaster, organic paint and an exterior cladding made from locally grown sweet-chestnut trees. Underfloor heating was installed beneath the exposed-screed floors, and discreet solar panels have been inserted into the roof.

Nevis House

Julian Arendt Associates

Nevis, St Kitts and Nevis, West Indies

14

This house was designed for a couple who had relocated from London to the Caribbean island of Nevis. Set on a sloping site with views to both the sea and the island's mountain, the home is a contemporary interpretation of the local vernacular in both style and materials. The building cascades down the hillside in such a way that it appears on approach to be a modest single-storey dwelling, while at the back it becomes a double-height volume. Large glazed doors in the rear façade lead to a series of terraces and balconies. Local building elements, such as fortified stone walls and the tin-clad roof, were selected not only as a contextual reference but also so that any hurricane damage can be repaired locally. The interior spaces surround a double-height living area, which provides a dramatic focal point and encourages cool breezes to circulate. Deep overhangs shield the rooms from the strong Caribbean sun. This is a thoughtfully designed home that, despite its grand scale, slips unobtrusively into its surroundings.

Newington Green House

15

Prewett Bizley Architects
London, UK

Designed by the architect Graham Bizley as both his home and an office for Prewett Bizley Architects, this building is a thoughtful addition to the gritty streetscape of London's Newington Green. It is squeezed on to a scrap of land previously occupied by a burnt-out storage unit. While the nearby buildings informed the choice of brick, the irregular plot and rights of light affecting neighbouring homes dictated the three-storey-high, turret-topped form. Whereas the west façade relies on a glazed roof to provide natural light, the street façade is dominated by randomly spaced windows, including a studio strip window that wraps around a corner to give views of the street. The emphasis throughout is on simplicity and economy, with basic building materials and joints exposed. The ground floor consists of an open-plan living, dining and kitchen area. The bedroom and bathroom are above, and on top of these is the office. The fourth floor has a laundry area leading to a roof terrace. Linking the floors, and forming the building's central spine, is a latticed staircase crafted from plywood and Douglas fir.

Fastnet House

Scott Tallon Walker Architects
Kinsale, County Cork, Ireland

16

Scott Tallon Walker Architects designed Fastnet House to maximize the southwards views over Kinsale Harbour. The 575-square-metre (6910-sq.-ft) house replaces a 1960s building that formerly stood on this awkward sloping site. To secure planning permission, the architect created a two-storey building that digs deep into the ground to avoid obscuring the neighbours' views. The exterior materials include a living roof made of sedum plants, as well as cedar cladding, floor-to-ceiling glazing, painted steel, and stone walling that matches the rocks on the site. While the ground floor is constructed from concrete, the first-floor steel structure allowed the architects to avoid corner columns, thereby maximizing views through the living-room and kitchen windows, which stand 3 metres (10 ft) high. Additional spaces include four bedrooms, a separate apartment accessible both from the main house and from the outside, a swimming pool, a large games room and a barbecue area from which the owners can admire views across the water while entertaining their guests.

Kronenberg House

17

Tzannes Associates
Killcare, New South Wales, Australia

This holiday home perches on a steep slope overlooking the spectacular coastline of New South Wales. The zinc-clad box has two alternative identities. When the owners are absent, louvred metal shutters fold around the exterior to create a solid, silver mass among the trees, but when they are at home these louvres fold back to create an almost transparent viewing platform. Full-height glass doors stretch across the entire front of the building, offering panoramas of the ocean, while at the rear enormous swathes of glass walling interspersed with glass doors open up the interior to the surrounding bushland. Internally, the house consists of a single large space. Sliding plywood wall panels at each end can be closed to separate the sleeping areas from the central kitchen, living and dining area. One of these two sleeping areas is also used as a study and includes an ingenious desk that converts into a double bed. Although its design appears simple, this is a sophisticated building providing flexible living spaces that fully exploit the setting.

Lime House

Alan Power Architects
London, UK

18

This quirky Georgian house, with its façade of lime green, stands within a conservation area in London's Notting Hill. The owners commissioned the architect to rearrange the internal spaces to create an eye-catching, light-filled home. A central element in the new design was the replacement of the original dog-leg staircase with a laminated-glass stair enclosed by walls of glass. Along with the rooflight inserted along the length of the building, the stairwell admits natural light into what had been a gloomy interior. The top floor is given over to a large living-room, fitted with a new beech floor and with windows at the front and rear. Below is the kitchen and dining area, which was moved from the basement to the ground floor. Full-height glass doors at the back of the building lead to a terrace on the roof of a small extension. Limestone floors and stainless-steel kitchen units complete the modern makeover. The lower-ground floor now accommodates the bedrooms, including the master bedroom, which has a connecting dressing-room and bathroom in the rear extension.

Villa Le Beaucet

19

Jean-Paul Bonnemaison
Le Beaucet, Vaucluse, France

Crowned by a ruined twelfth-century castle, the ancient fortified village of Le Beaucet is perched on a hilltop in western Provence. Below the castle, narrow streets wind between a melange of stone buildings. At one end of the main street, not far from the church, the architect Jean-Paul Bonnemaison has designed a home that, while contemporary in style, captures the essence of the village. Built above the cellars of an old olive oil factory, the house is in two parts: a four-storey family residence and a two-storey building that accommodates the guest rooms and services. From the street side, these buildings are discreet and unobtrusive, their walls constructed from the mellow local stone. By contrast, the front façade of the main house is clad almost entirely in glass. This creates a vast interior atrium into which the architect inserted an open-tread staircase and a series of suspended landings. The design not only draws natural daylight into the core of the building but also allows the occupants uninterrupted enjoyment of the beautiful views.

New Pavilion

Knox Bhavan Architects
Nayland, Suffolk, UK

20

Standing on a hill in the north of the Stour valley in the Suffolk village of Nayland, the New Pavilion was designed by Knox Bhavan Architects to complement the neighbouring 1960s property. All the materials used for the exterior of the pavilion are from the same palette as those that appear in the original house, and the curved copper roof of the new structure follows the scallop-shaped roof of the old. Internally, the building comprises one large open space with a free-standing pod at its centre. This curvaceous installation, clad in weathered sycamore, constitutes the focus of the interior and accommodates a shower room, a storage cupboard and a galley kitchen that faces out into the main space. When open, the pod's sliding and pivoting doors carve the internal space into two separate rooms. The gable-end walls of the building are lined with shelving units finished in a range of contrasting veneers, while a glazed wall, with western red cedar boarding in the higher section of the façade, overlooks the garden.

VXO House

Alison Brooks Architects
London, UK

21

This strikingly original home incorporates three structures: the V-House, the X-Pavilion and the O-Port. A 1960s house was reconfigured on two floors to create a double-height glass gallery over the dining-room, connecting the living areas both horizontally and vertically as well as enhancing the relationship between interior and exterior spaces. The extension to the main house comprises a timber-clad box hovering above a glass-enclosed foyer. Three elements define this space: a suspended staircase encased by a stainless-steel mesh; a wall drawing by artist Simon Patterson, extending into the garden; and the supporting 'V' column, from which the name of the house is partly derived. Opposite the extension is a grass-roofed garden pavilion that functions as both a gymnasium and a guesthouse. Two of the façades are entirely glazed, exposing the X-shaped supporting column. The third structure is the carport at the entrance to the property. It has a timber roof held in place by stainless-steel frames and a single O-shaped support.

Yoyogi House

Waro Kishi and K. Associates/Architects

Tokyo, Japan

22

The irregular form of this house in a quiet residential district of Tokyo represents the architects' response to strict local planning regulations and the tight boundaries of the plot, which occupies 85 square metres (915 sq. ft). The four-storey building comprises a series of ambiguous, overlapping spaces amounting to 105 square metres (1130 sq. ft). The house is entered by means of an external staircase that climbs a metre (3 ft) above the sloping street. The main living spaces are arranged on this floor and include a kitchen, dining area and high-ceilinged living-room, which also functions as a gallery for the client, who is a paper-cutout artist. Glass doors slide back to open the ground floor to the terrace. Below is a basement garage, and above are the bedrooms and two further terraces. An eclectic combination of materials features in the exterior, including concrete, glass mosaic tiles, galbarium steel plate and bronze pane glass. These serve to highlight further the fragmented, box-like form of the building.

The Stables

Buckley Gray Yeoman
Suffolk, UK

23

The Stables is an L-shaped, red-brick former agricultural building in Suffolk converted into a home of 237 square metres (2551 sq. ft). Since it forms part of a farm complex, there were design constraints – for example, no windows could overlook adjacent buildings. The main circulation route therefore runs parallel to the rear walls, where views to the outside are restricted, allowing the main living spaces and bedrooms to be placed at the front, where large glass windows look out on to the garden. The ground floor comprises a series of open-plan spaces, partially divided by the original brick walls, new partitions and a free-standing bathroom pod. Zones are also demarcated by changes in roof volume. A double-height corridor, capped by a strip rooflight, runs the length of the two-storey section of the building, letting light into the centre of the home, while also linking the ground- and first-floor spaces. Bold in its use of both traditional and modern materials, The Stables preserves its agricultural character while providing a practical and light-filled modern home.

Club Row House

Thinking Space
London, UK

24

This compact 125-square-metre (1345-sq.-ft) building stands in a convenient spot on the northern outskirts of the City of London. Developers had previously disregarded the location because it was subject to right-of-light restrictions and a right of way existed across the site. The architect overcame these restraints imaginatively, creating a three-storey building that scoops in the maximum amount of natural light. The internal spaces are arranged around an atrium, which stretches the full height of the building, unifying the rooms and diffusing illumination from the rooflight above. The basement also benefits from a rooflight, slotted into the pavement, while the upper two storeys incorporate gigantic floor-to-ceiling windows overlooking the mature plane trees lining the street. Every last centimetre of indoor space is exploited, and a roof terrace provides an ample outdoor area. This once-neglected pocket of land now accommodates a sleek and surprisingly spacious urban home.

Yarrawa Hill

25

Jones Architecture
Robertson, New South Wales, Australia

This holiday home by architect Mark Jones floats on steel poles sunk deep into the rainforest floor. It is designed to connect its occupants with the surrounding landscape, while providing both open communal spaces and more secluded private areas. The building has three interconnecting parts, including two pavilions that jut out over a steep north-facing hillside. In the west pavilion is an open-plan area 12 metres (40 ft) wide, accommodating living, kitchen and dining spaces. This pitched-roofed room is wrapped in three walls of glass with doors giving access to two exterior decks. Below is a self-contained suite that was added later. A shelf-lined corridor links the principal living space to the east wing, where there are two bedrooms – both with en suite bathrooms and studies – and a conservatory that leads to another sprawling deck. Yarrawa Hill is a building that encapsulates a relaxed holiday spirit, while offering a variety of interior and exterior spaces from which guests can admire the view across the rainforest to the sea.

Gallery House

Charles Barclay Architects
Cumnor, Oxfordshire, UK

26

The owner of this Oxfordshire house commissioned Charles Barclay Architects to create a two-storey extension that would include a space for displaying his collection of Renaissance sculpture. The external appearance of the addition had to comply with local planning rules, and the architect designed a discreet façade that complements the existing building in both form and materials. The pinwheel plan, however, with four 'arms' leading from a central, flat-roofed room and gables on each elevation, made it possible to create a dramatic contemporary interior.

The principal exhibition space is a double-height void in which the owner's sixteenth-century chimneypiece made from Caen stone occupies centre stage. Within this space, at an upper level, is a gallery that includes a bedroom and bathroom, linked by a bridge to the first floor of the farmhouse. While the domestic spaces have reclaimed jarra-wood floors, the exhibition space is distinguished by reclaimed slate slabs, crisp white walls and grand proportions, perfectly setting off the sculpture collection.

Holland Park House

McLean Quinlan
London, UK

27

A decrepit Victorian villa in London's Notting Hill has been transformed into a luxurious, ultra-modern home. The client, a collector of Renaissance picture frames, commissioned the architect to create a home for a young family, incorporating a workspace, but he also requested the feel of a modern art gallery. In response, McLean Quinlan reconfigured the existing interior and added a two-storey extension to the rear. The centre of the house is now occupied by a four-storey-high atrium, capped with a dramatic glass roof and partly filled by a beautifully crafted cherrywood staircase. A children's playroom is located under the sloping eaves, while the first and second floors accommodate bedrooms and decadent bathrooms. Twin bureaux stand on either side of the generous entrance hall, and on the far side of the atrium lies a full-width drawing-room. The lower ground floor, which includes the housekeeper's quarters as well as an open-plan kitchen and living area overlooking the garden, has a more informal ambience. The detailing throughout is immaculate.

Bayview Avenue House

Luigi Rosselli Architects
Sydney, New South Wales, Australia

28

With its curved form and dazzling white walls, this house overlooking Sydney Harbour is reminiscent of the Modernist buildings of the 1930s. The architect, Luigi Rosselli, has drawn on elements from that era and combined them with innovative technology to create a comfortable home equipped for twenty-first-century living. Bayview Avenue House forms the western boundary of a corner plot, and internal spaces are arranged in linear fashion. At the northern end, the large master bedroom, with its own private balcony, has a view over the swimming pool to the harbour beyond. Another balcony, on the eastern side, connects with the two other bedrooms. Inside the house, a mixture of materials and colours creates distinct zones. The combined kitchen and dining area, which leads on to a stone terrace, is bright with accents of orange, while the informal living area has built-in wooden furniture and dark-crimson walls. Meticulously detailed and beautifully executed, this house proves how successfully a Modernist aesthetic can be when translated into a home of today.

Banham House

Ellis Miller
Cambridgeshire, UK

29

This elegant steel-and-glass house was commissioned by Mary Banham, the artist wife of the late Reyner Banham, one of Britain's most celebrated architectural critics. Seeming to hover above the soggy ground of the Cambridgeshire fens, the building draws heavily on the work of such American architects as Philip Johnson and Ludwig Mies van der Rohe. Yet it is also site-specific and designed precisely around the needs of its occupant. Mary Banham was attracted to the site by the quality of the light and the views of Ely Cathedral, and Ellis Miller capitalized on both these assets by encasing the building in swathes of glass. Inside, the single-storey home has unusually high ceilings and comprises a galley kitchen, shower room, sleeping area and large living space and studio. In summer, external venetian blinds keep the house cool, while in winter stored heat from the sun is released by the thermally massive concrete floor and a wall made of Braithwaite water-storage tanks. The client has stamped her own identity on the house, as the architect intended, by splattering paint on the industrial grey floors.

106

Pawson House

John Pawson
London, UK

This traditional nineteenth-century terraced house is located in a conservation area in west London. Its protected status meant that the architect John Pawson had to leave the façade untouched, but beyond the front door he transformed the property, stamping it with his signature pared-down and yet highly sophisticated style. The interiors were gutted and reconfigured to maximize the number and extent of unencumbered spaces. Incisions in the exterior shell allow natural light to penetrate deep into the building. At the rear of the house, an almost invisible glass partition obliterates the divide between inside and outdoor areas, while the extension of the kitchen counter into the paved garden enhances the impression of continuity. At the top of the house, a glazed slot running the length of the ceiling allows light to spill down a triple-height staircase. While the ultra-modern interior signals a radical departure from the traditional street façade, the old and new styles of architecture are united by a shared elegance.

108

Tuath na Mara

MacGabhann Architects
Lough Swilly, County Donegal, Ireland

31

This holiday home on Lough Swilly in County Donegal embodies a number of paradoxes. With its roof and walls clad in black zinc, the building exudes the same sense of permanence as the ancient rocks around it, while its huge panes of glass, making it at points almost transparent, give the impression of weightlessness and insubstantiality. Despite its strikingly modern appearance, the house, designed by MacGabhann Architects, has a floor plan inspired by Ireland's traditional narrow cottage, with rooms laid out in linear fashion on a north–south axis. In the middle of the building are three bedrooms and auxiliary spaces as well as a bookshelf-lined corridor that connects the living spaces at each end. The communal spaces are fully glazed, while the bedrooms have slit windows that give framed views of the landscape. Entering the house involves stepping over a gap between entrance ramp and front door. Reminiscent of stepping from a platform on to a train, this quirky device serves to remind the family that they have left ordinary life behind and have arrived at their holiday destination.

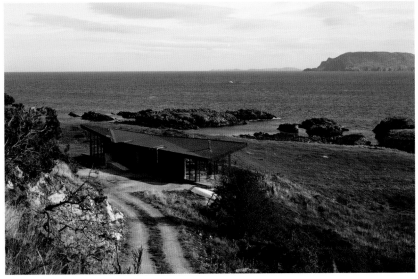

Sagaponac Pool House

Hariri & Hariri Architecture
Long Island, New York, USA

32

Sagaponac Pool House stands in 1 hectare (2.7 acres) of wooded countryside on New York's Long Island, between the districts of South Hampton and East Hampton, in a development of architect-designed houses (see also no. 59). Designed to interact with its surroundings, the minimalist structure rests on a platform within the untouched natural landscape and incorporates large expanses of glass, which frame the panoramic views. Covering an area of 423 square metres (4600 sq. ft), the house consists of two simple rectangular volumes, arranged in an L-shape around the outdoor swimming pool, multi-level terraces and covered porch with shower. This outdoor living space is accessible and visible from all other parts of the house and provides a useful extension to the property. Although remarkably transparent, the house can be made private by the closure of a series of metal shutters mounted on the exterior walls. The shutters not only provide security when the house is unoccupied but also give the owners the opportunity to reveal or conceal spaces within their home, depending on the occasion.

114

115

Car Designs House

Bere Architects
London, UK

33

This mews house occupies a small, wedge-shaped piece of land in a conservation area in Hampstead, north London. From the street, it is quintessentially English in appearance, with traditional brick walls and boxed windows, but hidden from the casual observer is the most dramatic element of the building: the rounded, glass-clad top floor that is set back from the line of the street. The curvaceous exterior geometry continues inside, where a flamboyant spiral staircase forms the spine of the building. The ground floor accommodates a double garage in addition to a galley kitchen and an open-plan living and dining area. Above this, cleverly arranged to complement the irregular floor plan, are three bedrooms, two bathrooms and a study. However, the most impressive room in the house is to be found at the very top, where a generously proportioned workspace, wrapped in glass, leads out on to a secluded roof terrace. Making imaginative use of an awkward plot, the architect has created a highly functional building that is full of surprises.

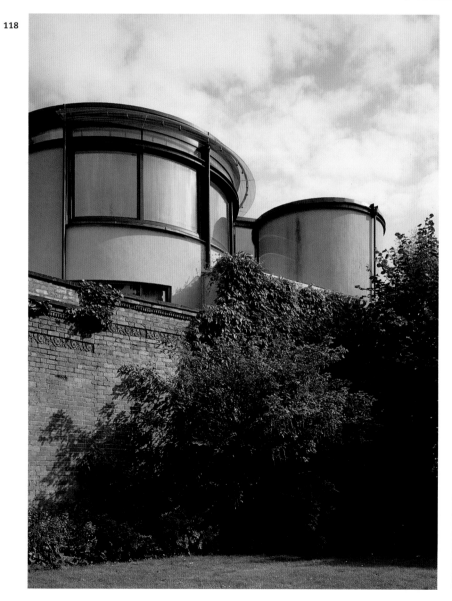

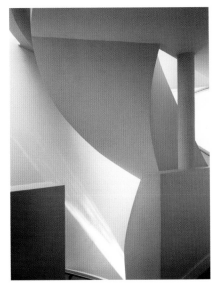

Check House 2

KNTA Architects
Singapore

34

This luxurious contemporary home stands on a sloping site near Singapore's botanical gardens, close to KNTA Architects' first Check House (built in 1994). Reached by a drive 100 metres (330 ft) long, the house is built to a skewed U-shaped plan around a sheltered garden with swimming pool and decked outdoor area. It is an intriguing mix of Western and Eastern influences: the crisp white exterior walls, large expanses of glass and variety of window shapes reflect an international Modernist style, but the double-skin roof – which includes a suspended metal layer to deflect heat from the top of the house and create a ventilation void – is a response to the climate. The interior is divided into three zones: a parents' wing, a family living area and a more public space for entertaining. The outdoor area for Chinese cooking linked to the kitchen is one Eastern touch; the dining-room walls, which are curved to accommodate a traditional circular Chinese dining-table, are another. In the basement, a cinema and gymnasium – once public spaces, now brought into the home – are a nod to more global trends.

Holly Barn

Knox Bhavan Architects
Reedham, Norfolk, UK

35

This striking wooden house on the Norfolk Broads is sensitive both to its setting and to the needs of its owners, one of whom uses a wheelchair. It replaces a dilapidated barn, and the form and materials of the building take inspiration from the local vernacular of windmills and boathouses. The detailing is meticulous: for example, the hidden gutter allows the curved eaves to connect seamlessly with the Siberian larch cladding. Inside, rooms are arranged in a linear fashion. The ground floor accommodates the entrance hall, four guest bedrooms, two bathrooms and a playroom. The first floor, which has spectacular panoramic views, is reserved for the open-plan kitchen and dining area, living-room, master bedroom, study and bathroom. Of these rooms, only the bathroom is fully enclosed; the upper sections of the remaining partition walls are made from glass, creating the sense of one continuous space. The proportions of the hallways and rooms were carefully considered to accommodate the turning circle of a wheelchair, and the rounded corners of walls and furniture echo the curves of the exterior.

Mews House

Piers Ford Architects
London, UK

36

A notorious drawback of the traditional mews house is the lack of natural daylight that results from having only one windowed façade. Piers Ford Architects has found an inventive solution to this problem in its remodelling of a twenty-year-old mews property in London's King's Cross district. The most distinctive feature of the house is the generous amount of glazing that has been used both externally and internally. An enormous sliding glass roof inserted over the double-height living-room creates the effect of an internal courtyard.

When open, this rooflight serves as a canopy to an al-fresco dining space on the newly created roof terrace. The installation of this roof gave the clients the advantage of two flexible rooms that can be either enclosed or exposed to the elements. The internal layout of the property was rearranged to accommodate an additional bedroom and a study, while new windows with galvanized-steel frames and lintels in the front elevation give a contemporary appearance.

Arkö Summer House

37

Marge Arkitekter
Sweden

Apparently balancing on a rock plinth, this summer home is a subtle addition to the eastern coastline of Sweden. The house occupies a total of 60 square metres (646 sq. ft) and comprises two volumes, slightly separated in plan and section to create a south-west-facing terrace with views to the sea and a more private terrace that catches the morning sun. Stone steps lead down to a timber jetty. The interior space is divided into a bedroom, an open-plan kitchen and living-room, a dining area, a bathroom and a sauna. The light painted walls and

dark wooden floors create a clean, sophisticated appearance. By contrast, the exterior is clad in larch planks and the house has a moss-covered roof. Over time, it will weather and blend into the barren landscape.

134

136

Esher House

Wilkinson King Architects
Esher, Surrey, UK

38

This five-bedroomed family home is situated on the northern boundary of a large, mature, secluded garden in Surrey. A brick-faced wall wraps around two sides of the rectangular building, enclosing the ground-floor living spaces and the swimming pool and pool house to the rear. Large swathes of glass on the other two façades offer views south over the garden and connect the living spaces with the pool and extensive patio area. By contrast, the first floor, which contains the five bedrooms, each with en suite bathroom, is more enclosed,

its rooms shielded behind white-rendered walls. The exception is the master bedroom, which has an east-facing wall of glass overlooking the swimming pool. The architect gave high priority to maximizing the amount of natural light that enters the house. A glass-capped double-height atrium with a transparent staircase makes it possible for light to penetrate into the centre of the building. The decorative scheme is simple and white throughout to enhance the effects of light and space.

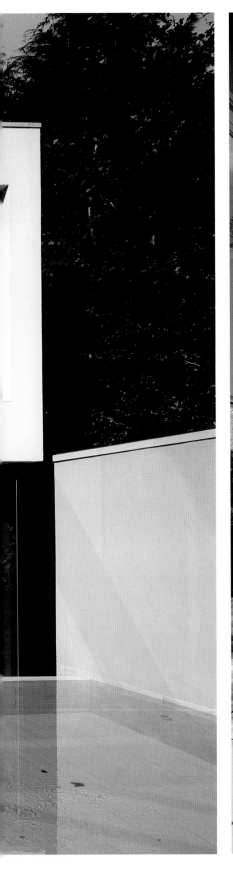

Max Burt House

ACQ
London, UK

39

This modern two-storey home, part of a development of a factory site in London's Ladbroke Grove, is a visual treat that abounds in rich, textured materials. It is also a clever adaptation of a building to meet the needs of a wheelchair-bound client. Seriously injured in a car crash at the age of thirty-four, the owner employed architect ACQ (now part of FLACQ) to design the space for his needs. His wife, interior designer Lucy Eadie, created the overall look. The back of the property was removed and replaced with a glass lift. Doorways were adapted and work surfaces commissioned to be exactly the right height. A state-of-the-art computer system allows the owner to adjust the heating and lighting, open windows and doors and play music at the touch of a button. The lower floor consists of an open-plan kitchen, living and dining area, which receives generous natural daylight through the partially glazed roof. The upstairs rooms are cosier, including a bedroom featuring black American walnut panels and a bathroom with marble floors, mosaic walls and a two-way mirror that allows light from the skylight to penetrate to the shower behind.

Juicy House

Atelier Bow-Wow

Tokyo, Japan

40

The Setagaya ward, close to central Tokyo, is densely populated and subject to stringent rules about building height. When local architect Atelier Bow-Wow was commissioned to build the Juicy House on a plot of 42.29 square metres (455¼ sq. ft), maximizing living space in a compact shell was the main aim. The interior is arranged over four floors linked by a delicate open-tread staircase. The bedrooms and a study are sunk at basement level, below a library, and above that is a second-floor kitchen, living and dining area. The planning code meant that the top floor could cover only half of the building's footprint and must be used for 'non-livable' purposes, so a bathroom with a large balcony was installed there. Rather than waste space with internal partition walls, the architect used colours to demarcate different areas. The entrance is bright pink, the bedrooms are a more subdued pale yellow, the library is white and the second floor a bold orange. The brightly hued walls create a stark contrast with the cutaway windows, which have been positioned to frame views of surrounding buildings.

148

Cottage Extension

Mitchell Taylor Workshop

Bath, Somerset, UK

41

Flanked by trees but offering sweeping views of the valley below, this secluded house near Bath, in the west of England, has two parts: a crenellated stone gamekeeper's cottage dating from 1786 and a modern linear extension. Since there is no car access, the owners must walk 400 metres (440 yds) through woodland from the road to the front door. The low-budget home was designed for his family by the architect Piers Taylor of Mitchell Taylor Workshop, who chose to leave exposed the utilitarian materials used in its construction. Shuttering ply was used for the walls and the frame was made of local green oak. Stainless-steel bolts punctuate the external skin, and much of the exterior is clad in dark-grey corrugated sheets, echoing the Dutch barns common to the area. The old cottage accommodates the staircase and a snug living-room and guest bedroom, while the extension has an open-plan living, kitchen and dining area and, above, bedrooms divided simply by sliding partition walls. Although the contrast between the two parts of the house could not be starker, they are unified by the honest display of materials.

Highgate House

Eldridge Smerin

London, UK

42

This house in Highgate village, north London, designed by Eldridge Smerin, was shortlisted for the coveted Stirling Prize and won a Royal Institute of British Architects award in 2001. Surprisingly, given its ultra-modern appearance, the house is actually a reworking of a 1950s detached residence. While the core of the building remains, the internal area has been doubled by the addition of three glass volumes – two on the sides of the building and one on the top, replacing the previous pitched roof and creating a room that fully exploits the views. These additions made possible the creation of three double-height atria and encouraged natural light to penetrate deep into the interiors. The internal spaces are divided into four zones: one for children, one for adults, one for all the family and, on the top floor, a work studio. Sliding and folding doors allow these zones to be kept separate from one another or to be connected. From the exposed concrete walls to the bespoke furniture, the detailing is immaculate. Every single aspect of this project is carefully considered and successfully executed.

South Melbourne House

43

Tom Isaksson Architect

South Melbourne, Victoria, Australia

Dating originally from the 1860s, South Melbourne House had a new chapter added to its history in 2006 with the completion of an extension by the architect Tom Isaksson. From the exterior, the two parts of the house are noticeably different, but they are sympathetic to each other. Reclaimed bricks were chosen for the ground floor and copper cladding for the upper level of the extension. The earthy tones of both will become more muted with age to complement the existing structure. Bridging the two sections is a strip of glass that draws light into the centre of the building. Only the top panel, which glows bright red, hints at the bold colour scheme inside. The interiors have been reorganized to make large rooms that flow into one another. The kitchen and dining area in the extension opens to the garden through folding glass doors. While the walls are white and the floors a grey basalt throughout, the house is punctuated by furnishings and decorative touches in primary colours. This modern scheme unites the whole and provides a startling contrast to the house's subdued external appearance.

Mews Housing

De Blacam & Meagher Architects
Dublin, County Dublin, Ireland

44

Three terraced houses are squeezed on to a restricted plot in a back lane in Dublin. The houses are unashamedly modern, constructed from a palette of concrete, brick, oak, plaster and copper. The vaulted copper-clad roofs give them their distinctive form. Each building is long and narrow, measuring 4 metres (13 ft) in width and varying in depth from 12 to 15 metres (39 to 49 ft). The living spaces are spread over three floors, with the bedrooms on the ground and top floors and the open-plan living, kitchen and dining areas sandwiched between.

Generously proportioned windows admit light into the buildings, and apertures cut from the internal portioning walls allow that light to be diffused throughout the three floors. The interior design maximizes the available floor space by means of such clever storage solutions as built-in shelves and benches that double as cupboards. The development demonstrates how even the smallest of plots can be successfully exploited to provide comfortable contemporary homes.

The Retreat

Buckley Gray Yeoman
Norfolk, UK

45

The Retreat is an entirely new type of holiday home. Conceived by the British architect Buckley Gray Yeoman, it is built not only in a modern style, with spacious and stylish interiors, but also from environmentally friendly materials. Retreat houses, which are prefabricated and come in a range of different models, are constructed from timber certified by the Forest Stewardship Council. The floors are solid oak, the carpets are 100 per cent wool, and the glazing is encased in hardwood frames. Optional sustainable extras include sheep's-wool insulation, grass roofs, photovoltaic solar panels and rainwater-collection systems. The Retreat is available with either a flat or a pitched roof, and with two or three bedrooms. It includes teak wood in the kitchen and bathroom, and Bosch kitchen appliances. Retreat homes have already begun to appear in holiday parks across the UK, and they are being exported to France, Spain and Italy. As an increasing number of people seek to take more environmentally friendly holidays, the popularity of The Retreat and similar sustainable models looks set to soar.

Ealing House

McLean Quinlan

London, UK

46

McLean Quinlan has transformed this Edwardian two-storey brick house in Ealing, west London, into a light-filled modern home for a young family. An extension to the rear, stretching across almost the entire width of the house, incorporates sleek sliding glass doors, which connect the newly created dining and living areas to a paved terrace. The footprint of the upper floors is unchanged, although crisp white rendering and the addition of large panes of glass give the building a contemporary facelift. In addition to the bedrooms on the first floor, the upper attic level was radically rearranged to provide a light-filled master bedroom suite and study. The neutral decorative scheme throughout the building enhances the effect of natural light, while clever storage solutions, such as bespoke units slotted into the eaves in the study, allow the family to keep their home free of clutter.

Howth House

47

O'Donnell & Tuomey Architects
Howth, County Dublin, Ireland

Designed from the inside out, Howth House exploits to the full both the views and the quality of light in its coastal location. The house is set halfway up a hill, overlooking Howth Harbour and the sea beyond. It is orientated towards the north, so that the seascape can be observed away from the sun's glare. While glazing on the southern façade lets light diffuse through the building, it is the extensive panes of glass on the north side that are the main feature and frame the views. Having previously lived in a nearby Victorian villa with conventional living spaces, the clients wanted a more informal layout better suited to modern family life. Howth House consists of free-flowing, sculptural spaces with the dining-room table as its focus. Materials throughout are rich in texture and colour: concrete ceilings are boardmarked to match the pattern of the floorboards; timber floors are extended vertically at the edges to create partitions and balustrades; and the skylit shower rooms are tiled in glass mosaics. The austerity of the plain walls in the main spaces serves to magnify the impact of the views.

Vaucluse House 2

JAHN Associates
Sydney, New South Wales, Australia

48

This luxurious five-bedroomed house is one of two properties by JAHN Associates on an unusual site beside Vaucluse Bay in Sydney Harbour (the other is no. 83). The land was previously occupied by a 1960s Modernist box, which could not be fully demolished because of the fragile state of its foundations. Instead, the roof and lightweight walls were removed, the existing building was lowered by one floor, a new bedroom level was added above the existing garage, and additional levels were built on the side of the property. Inside, the floors are arranged to reflect the various activities that take place in the household, with the children's area below and the adult and entertainment spaces sited on the upper level to take full advantage of the views. The most impressive room is the formal living area, where the glazed walls open up to extend the living space on to a sprawling terrace. Furnishings throughout are sleek and contemporary as befits such a startlingly modern home.

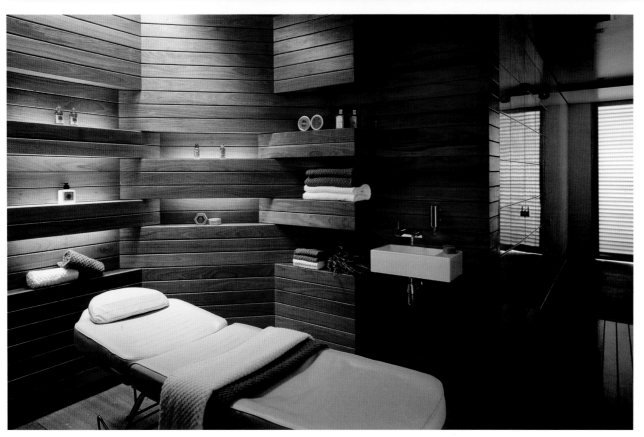

Reutter House

49

Mathias Klotz
Cachagua, Valparaíso, Chile

The Reutter House stands on a hillside close to Cachagua beach in Chile, some 140 kilometres (87 miles) from the capital, Santiago. The surrounding pine trees inspired the form and materials of the building. Jutting out over a steep slope, the house consists of two rectangular volumes set on a concrete plinth. The larger of the volumes is clad in wood and the smaller in copper. The house is reached from the rear by a 30-metre (100-ft) bridge that meanders through the trees. A large roof terrace on top of the building has wonderful ocean views, and from here a steel staircase leads down, first to a covered terrace and then inside the building. Instead of interior doors, there are large sliding partitions that allow an open or closed arrangement of the rooms. A concrete service core cuts through the centre of the house and encases the staff bedroom and laundry at ground-floor level, the kitchen and television room on the second floor, and the study on the third. As on the exterior, the materials are left raw and exposed to complement the natural setting.

Holland Park House

ACQ
London, UK

50

ACQ (now part of FLACQ) remodelled this large west London town house to create a luxurious home characterized by light-filled, free-flowing living spaces. Since the house is located within a conservation area, there were restrictions on the alterations that could be made. The main thrust of the work was carried out at the rear, with the addition of a lower-ground-floor extension that stretches across the entire width of the property. Into this the architect inserted a large family area with an open-plan kitchen, living and dining area. Sliding full-height glass doors lead on to a large sunken terrace, while circular rooflights draw in additional natural light. More formal living areas are on the ground floor, with a clever frameless bay window providing views of the garden and a glass door leading on to the newly created balcony. Space is maximized throughout by building in shelves, storage units and entertainment systems, such as the television. The once-dated house has retained its charm while receiving a very modern makeover.

178

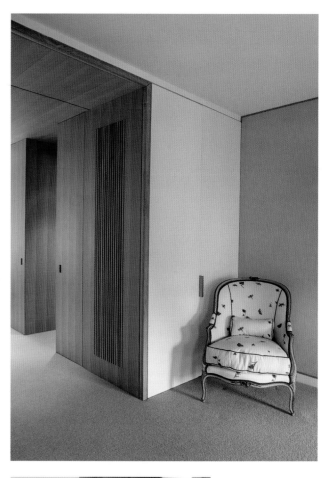

Long House

51

Grafton Architects

Dublin, County Dublin, Ireland

This modern mews house stands on a narrow lane leading off a leafy canalside terrace. Faced with a small and introverted plot, the architect devised an unusual solution. The house occupies the entire 6.5 × 20-metre (21 × 66-ft) site and comprises a series of linked internal and external spaces. While the perimeter walls are mostly made of solid masonry, wood and glass form the interior partitioning walls. From the street, the building resembles a fortress: apart from a vertical strip of brick, it is covered with chunky wooden cladding. The top section of the façade consists of timber panels interspersed with air gaps, partially concealing the balcony behind. As you make your way around the house, you come across a series of such outdoor spaces, each acting as a light well and ingeniously introducing more natural illumination into the home. The interior wall-finishes are exposed, and the minimalist wooden furniture complements the spareness of the overall design.

182

Uplands

52

Freeland Rees Roberts Architects
Suffolk, UK

Surrounded by the beautiful countryside of the Shotley peninsula in Suffolk, this house incorporates elements of the farmhouse that it replaced while providing a bright and open contemporary living space. The floor plan of the three-bedroomed house is similar to that of its predecessor, but the exterior comprises a melange of shapes and materials. From the brick-clad ground floor, generous glazed apertures offer views of the surrounding oak trees and apple orchards. To the east, beyond a green-oak pergola, is a Japanese tea house, while to the west stands a single-storey billiard room lit by windows in the butterfly-shaped roof. Above, the two main bedrooms occupy wedge-shaped structures clad in oak and roofed with sheets of copper. The slant of the roof makes it possible to accommodate double-height, fully glazed façades with connecting balconies. Other sections of the first floor are clad in traditional hung tiles. The eclectic choice of materials enabled the architect to create a house that, while daring in form, is subtle in appearance.

186

The Red House

Patricia Miyamoto
Alpes-Maritimes, France

53

Perched on a hill above the Côte d'Azur, the Red House was designed to include stepped outdoor terraces that exploit the astounding views. The style of the building was informed partly by the traditional *mas*, or simple farmhouse, and partly by local planning regulations, which decree that all new-build houses must have terracotta roofs with a 30-degree pitch. The thick load-bearing walls have a high thermal mass, keeping the building cool during the day and releasing the warmth of the walls at night, as in a traditional *mas*. After six months of experimentation, burgundy was chosen for the colour of the walls because it complemented so well the surrounding olive grove. Extending over 200 square metres (2153 sq. ft), the interior feels light and spacious owing to ceiling heights of 3 metres (10 ft) and tall, narrow windows. Interior and exterior flooring, kitchen counters, bathrooms and interior benches are of a local ivory-coloured limestone, which provides a richly textured yet subtle backdrop to the owner's collection of modernist furniture and contemporary art.

Dulwich Pool House

ACQ
London, UK

54

This elegant urban villa in Dulwich, a leafy suburb in south London, built in the early years of the twentieth century, has been transformed by the addition of a glass-encased extension and dramatic swimming pool to the rear. The architect ACQ (now part of FLACQ) opened up the entire ground floor, creating a view from the front door across the kitchen, dining and living areas to the pool beyond, and rendering the ground-floor space more flexible and convenient. The impact of the pool is heightened by the decision to paint the walls that separate it from the rest of the garden in a bold pink. Both the water and the retaining walls can be lit at night, enhancing the impression that the pool and its terrace are an extension of the main living areas of the stylish home.

Cardy Net House

Hurd Rolland

Lower Largo, Fife, UK

55

This striking contemporary seaside home has a fascinating history. The first building on the site was constructed in 1867 as a fishing-net factory to service the thriving herring industry in the Scottish village of Lower Largo. The factory proved so successful that its owner was able to build a Victorian villa with a large walled garden, incorporating the original structure. In 2000 the current owners, architects Mike and Liz Rolland, began converting it into a spacious, light-filled home with six bedrooms. The Grade B-listed factory, which had been derelict for a century, had to be stripped back to its bare bricks in order to eradicate the damp, but the layout of the interior has been left largely unchanged. Bedrooms and bathrooms are located on the outside edges of the building, where storerooms and managers' offices once were. The open-plan living, dining and kitchen area is arranged within the cavernous central core. Sliding glass doors along the south elevation give access to the sheltered terrace and provide the living area with extensive views of the sea.

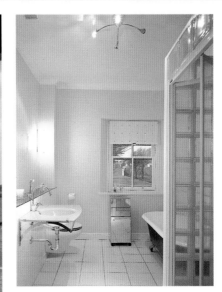

Katsura House

56

Keith Pike Associates
Sydney, New South Wales, Australia

Keith Pike, the owner and architect of this house in Sydney, is half-Japanese and studied at the Tokyo Institute of Technology. The design of his home is therefore strongly influenced by traditional Japanese architecture, although it has been modified to create a contemporary building well suited to the Australian climate and lifestyle. The house consists of a series of light-filled spaces with far-reaching views. On the ground floor, bedrooms are arranged around a central entrance hall and stairwell. Visible from this space, which is encased by frameless full-height glazing, are a rectangular koi pond at the front and a sunken plunge pool at the rear. The living and dining areas are on the first floor, with north and south walls of glass opening on to large balconies. A master bedroom on the third floor is designed with a scooped roof to draw in additional light. The interiors are bright and airy, with white walls and limestone floors. Contemporary versions of sliding Japanese *shoji* screens, made from rice paper sandwiched between layers of glass, and western red cedar screens add a further Eastern accent.

Family House

MMM Architects

Chislehurst, Kent, UK

57

Originally built in the 1920s, this family house in Kent had been extended piecemeal over the decades but lacked a clear identity and a cohesive internal space. The present owners therefore commissioned MMM Architects to refurbish and enlarge the building. A rear extension was constructed and several glass façades inserted to connect the property more harmoniously with the surrounding garden and to introduce greater quantities of natural light. Walls and floors were removed from the interior of the old building and the space

reconfigured to create generous double-height voids and a more practical layout, consisting of a series of open-plan living spaces. Interior finishes were upgraded to include timber floors, crisp white walls and ultra-modern built-in lighting. The result is a luxurious family home with large, well-lit spaces and a strong, unified character.

Focus House

Bere Architects

London, UK

58

Focus House, an energy-efficient home designed by Bere Architects on a triangular site in north London, incorporates stacked zinc-clad blocks punctuated with large plates of glass. The west elevation, on the street side, is a mere 2.8 metres (9 ft) wide, while at the rear the building widens to 7 metres (23 ft). The cascading arrangement of the boxes maximizes solar gain through the glass areas while demarcating internal spaces. On the ground floor is an open-plan kitchen, dining and living area with sliding doors to the garden. Stairs lead to the first floor, which has two children's bedrooms, a bathroom and a study that juts out over the front entrance; the master bedroom and bathroom are on the second floor. The design draws on the PassivHaus energy-saving principles, developed in Germany, and, as well as being well insulated, is airtight, thanks to meticulous detailing and high-quality windows from Scandinavia. Solar thermal panels are attached to the south elevation, and a heat-recovery system channels fresh air into the building while regulating the internal temperature.

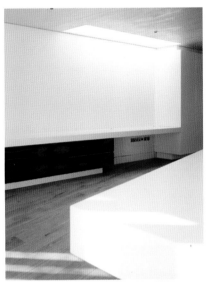

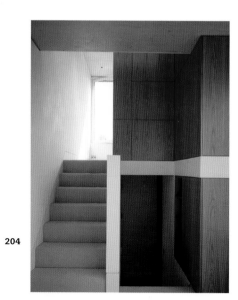

204

Sagaponac House

Selldorf Architects

Long Island, New York, USA

This 1380-square-metre (15,000-sq.-ft) home is one of thirty-four houses being built on 32.5 hectares (80 acres) of land in Sagaponac, Long Island. The developer commissioned a host of well-known architects, including Philip Johnson and Zaha Hadid, to create a collection of unique and exciting modern homes (see also no. 32). On Selldorf Architects' allocated plot, minimalist design and swathes of glass intertwine interior and exterior living spaces and connect the occupants with the landscape. A series of outdoor 'rooms' was created around the building:

to the south is a formal lawn with a raised terrace and pool; to the west is a sunken flower garden; to the north is an apple orchard reached across the front yard. The indoor living spaces are connected to the outdoors by a glass-flanked courtyard at the centre of a single-storey wing accommodating the hall, kitchen and living and dining areas. The adjacent two-storey wing offers elevated views from the bedrooms and terraces. The result is an elegant, well-proportioned home at peace with its surroundings.

Crescent House

Make

Calne, Wiltshire, UK

Ken Shuttleworth, the founder of Make architects, designed this distinctive house in Wiltshire as a country retreat for himself and his family. It consists of two crescent-shaped forms connected by a curving corridor, which doubles as a gallery and stretches the length of the building. The bedrooms, bathrooms and private living areas are located in the outer crescent, the solid convex wall of which shelters the house from the nearby road, while the inner crescent contains the open-plan living, kitchen and dining areas. The concave wall of the inner crescent is made from full-height panes of glass, allowing the early-morning sun to penetrate and giving an uninterrupted view of the garden. The arms of the inner crescent extend to wrap around the edges of the garden, framing the view and offering additional privacy. By abandoning the conventional box-like form of domestic buildings the architect has created a unique home, which, while striking in appearance, also provides bright, practical living spaces well shielded from the eyes of passers-by.

South Hill Park House

Robert Dye Associates
London, UK

61

An Edwardian semi-detached home in north London has been revived by the addition of three new volumes that both extend the floor area and transform the house's relationship with the rear garden and the sky. A new mansard roof at third-floor level provides two children's bedrooms, a family bathroom and a terrace, subtly hidden behind the front parapet. At the rear of the house, two interlocked timber-framed boxes, clad in stained wood, jut out dramatically into the garden. On the ground floor, a living area opens along its southern side through folding glass doors on to a decked terrace. A circular rooflight further brightens the space, and slot windows give framed views of the garden. Beneath this room is a pre-cast-concrete wine cellar. The second cube, at first-floor level, extends from the master bedroom and provides a luxurious en suite bathroom. While the end screen is made from sandblasted glass, additional slot windows offer views over both the neighbouring gardens and the London cityscape beyond.

Y House

Kei'ichi Irie + Power Unit Studio
Chita, Aichi, Japan

62

Y House occupies a hillside plot of 325 square metres (3500 sq. ft) between two suburban houses in Chita, Japan. The architect Kei'ichi Irie of Power Unit Studio is dismayed by the spread of closely packed housing on the outskirts of Japan's towns and cities and has made it his mission to design buildings that tread lightly on the ground, while creating living spaces with visual links to what remains of the natural landscape. He therefore left the gradient of the site unaltered, and Y House stands on a narrow concrete perch that encloses a bedroom at basement level.

From the street the house looks small and squat, with only a translucent glass entrance door and a picture window addressing its neighbours. At the back, by contrast, jutting out over the hillside, is a cantilevered frame accommodating a living area with a panorama across the nearby forest and valley. The sloping sides block out the surrounding buildings from sight. A large glass door with a heavy black border frames the view, while also providing access to the suspended terrace. A bathroom and study slot into the connecting tower at the side.

215

217

Hodges Place

63

Knox Bhavan Architects

Offham, Kent, UK

Knox Bhavan Architects has enlarged this seventeenth-century timber-framed farmhouse in Kent by constructing a contemporary but contextual extension. Set in the old kitchen garden, the linear addition is enclosed along one side by an old ragstone wall. This same wall is left exposed throughout the interior and offers a textural contrast to the smooth timber floors and cherry-veneer partition walls. The flat roof is planted with grass, to integrate the building further with its setting. Large sliding windows face the garden, which is divided from the extension by a long, narrow pool, and light bounces off the water to create a dappled effect on the ceilings. The space accommodates a kitchen, dining area, book-lined study and bathroom, arranged in a linear fashion. The understated design using site-sensitive materials complements the existing house and allows the owners to feel more closely connected with the garden.

Szirtes House

Chenchow Little Architects

Sydney, New South Wales, Australia

64

Despite being occupied by a family with two young children, this small Australian home is a model of calm. From the outside it resembles a solid black mass floating on a translucent base. The ground floor is almost entirely wrapped in floor-to-ceiling walls of glass, most sections of which can be slid back to dissolve the boundary between the building and its encircling terrace. Rooms are arranged according to a U-plan, with a lone Japanese maple planted in the central courtyard. To one side is the formal living-room, framed by black bamboo, and to the other is an open-plan living, kitchen and dining area. This arrangement makes it possible to look right through the building. When privacy is required, soft white drapes, which billow in the wind, can be drawn along each side. The upstairs bedrooms and bathrooms give even more privacy, although large windows sheltered by exterior blinds slice through the façades. The house is meticulously furnished and includes beautifully crafted woodwork, stone surfaces and crisp white walls. It is a restful space, but also a practical and flexible family home.

220

Notting Hill House

Found Associates

London, UK

65

Many of the streets of London's Notting Hill are lined with grand Victorian town houses, the original layouts of which comprised formal rooms connected by space-consuming corridors. In this 204-square-metre (2200-sq.-ft) house, the internal spaces were rearranged by Found Associates to create a soaring double-height atrium and a series of light-filled interconnected rooms. By stripping away the old rear façade and replacing it with large areas of glass on both the ground and the first floors, the architect introduced a remarkable amount of natural light, and, by removing many of the internal walls, allowed that light to reach the heart of the home. The double-height void at the centre, with its imposing modern chandelier, forms a link between the open-plan kitchen, dining and living areas. Bedrooms and bathrooms occupy the upper floors. By selecting a restricted palette of dark-stained timber and neutral walls, the architect created a unified design that offers flexible living spaces incorporating both private retreats and large rooms for entertaining.

226

Tidebrook Manor

ORMS

East Sussex, UK

66

The architectural and design practice ORMS has reorganized, extended and completely renovated this country estate, at the centre of which is a listed manor house with medieval origins. Several additional buildings, including a timber-framed barn, have been constructed over the centuries. The architect has transformed the whole property into a series of contemporary but character-filled living spaces. The barn, for example, which retains its exposed timber beams and roof trusses, now accommodates the games room. A modern extension provides the owners with an up-to-date kitchen including a sleek central island and built-in wooden storage units. This space is connected to the garden terrace by means of floor-to-ceiling glass doors. By sensitively restoring the old sections of the house and yet daring to introduce modern elements, the architect has opened a successful new chapter in the story of this historic home.

228

Bondi Beach House

67

Architects Johannsen + Associates
Sydney, New South Wales, Australia

Set on a hillside overlooking Sydney's Bondi Beach, this four-bedroomed house was designed by Architects Johannsen + Associates to take maximum advantage of the view. Arranged over five split levels, it has a total floor area of 300 square metres (3230 sq. ft). While the two lower floors accommodate the garage and sleeping quarters, the master bedroom is at the top, with the living areas sandwiched in between. This arrangement allows views through the building – from the loggia and swimming pool at the rear to the outdoor terrace laid out above the garage at the front. Both the west-facing front façade and the east-facing rear façade are clad predominantly in glass, with deep recesses and overhangs to reduce solar impact. Glass doors leading to the street-facing and rear reception rooms can be opened to encourage a natural cross-breeze. The interiors are simple and bright, with smooth polished-concrete floors, grey ironbark stair treads and walls painted in neutral tones. Imbued with a relaxed, contemporary feel, the house both complements and exploits its setting.

232

Portobello Road Houses

68

Alan Power Architects
London, UK

These two adjoining houses cleverly make the most of a small plot in London's Notting Hill. The site was excavated to create three-storey homes with front doors set back from the street at first-floor level; that made it possible to create two ground-floor bedrooms with full-height glass doors leading to small courtyards at the rear. The first floor contains an entrance hall, stairs, a third bedroom, and a kitchen and dining area with access to a rear balcony; a metal lattice grating covering half the balcony floor lets light filter through to the courtyards below. The gull-wing roof allowed the architect to glaze the walls on three sides of the top-floor living area, providing impressive amounts of natural light. This floor steps back to create a balcony at the front. Diffusion of light through the interiors is encouraged by open-tread staircases and glass balustrades, and rotating vertical wooden screens set into the front walls of the building can be adjusted to vary the amount of interaction that the owners have with the street.

234

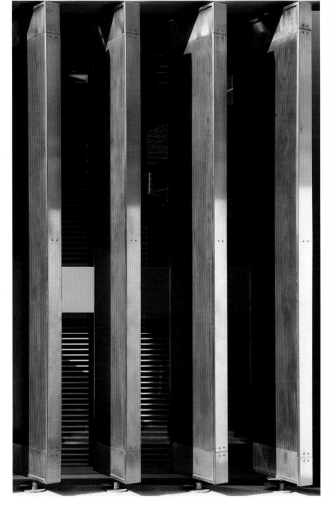

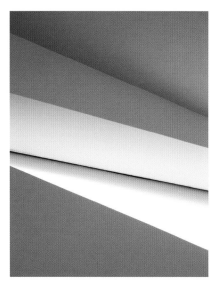

Ring House

TNA

Karuizawa, Nagano, Japan

69

The Ring House represents a masterclass in how to transform an undesirable plot of land into a unique and innovative contemporary home. Located in the Karuizawa forest some 300 kilometres (185 miles) north-west of Tokyo, the holiday home stands on a dark, north-facing, sloping site encircled by trees. Undeterred by these difficult conditions, the architect built a three-storey tower with the basement level semi-submerged below ground and the upper two floors wrapped in alternating layers of glass and timber. The solid-timber rings are carefully positioned to delineate areas of private space and to conceal such furnishings as kitchen cabinets, beds and bathroom fixtures. The glass sections admit surprisingly large amounts of natural light while constantly connecting the occupants to the forest. An open-tread staircase with narrow steel supports maximizes the impression of transparency. The Ring House is an ethereal home that almost dissolves into its surroundings.

Cookson–Smith House

70

Edward Cullinan Architects
Twickenham, Middlesex, UK

Situated on the bank of the River Thames in Twickenham, south-west London, this house takes full advantage of its watery outlook through the clever design of a series of unconventional interior and exterior spaces. Constructed from a combination of London stock brick, western red cedar and zinc cladding, the building is set back from the public road, to which it is linked by a driveway. As one enters the house, the river is immediately visible because the entrance hall is linked by a glass door to an external timber deck that stretches down to the water.

The rest of the house comprises three bedrooms and a series of eating, cooking and living spaces arranged around a central curved wall that incorporates stairs, storage and display cases. Various double-height voids inserted into the floor plan create a stepped arrangement of rooms, and large expanses of glazing on the river-facing façade frame the captivating views.

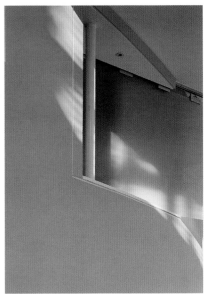

Cargo Fleet

Chance de Silva Architects

London, UK

71

The inspiration for this London house – which takes its name from an abandoned railway station between Redcar and Middlesbrough – is the industrial landscape of northern England, where the architect Steven Chance spent his childhood. Located on a corner plot, the building is a collage of industrial materials. The rusting Cor-ten steel panels that cover much of the exterior are counterpointed by rough-sawn larch cladding and cage-like metal balconies and window frames. The industrial theme continues inside, where concrete floors and exposed grey plaster contrast with shiny wooden panelling and floor-to-ceiling windows. In the glass-encased stairwell, the brick wall of the adjoining property is exposed. The house has two parts, linked by an enclosed walkway, which allows for flexible use in the future. Either it could be made into two separate living spaces or one part could be an annexe for an elderly relative, for example. The house pays homage to the disappearing industrial architecture of England; yet, despite its gritty palette of materials, it still provides a bright and comfortable home.

245

72

Forbes Street House

Smart Design Studio
Darlinghurst, New South Wales, Australia

From the street, this terraced house looks no different from its neighbours, but it has been comprehensively remodelled inside, and a tower-like extension has been constructed at the rear of the building. The new structure was designed to accommodate a basement, which has been slotted under the stone-paved courtyard; a kitchen on the ground floor; a bathroom on the first floor; and a roof terrace at the top. To make up for the restricted size of the extension, the architect, Smart Design Studio, incorporated clever space-saving solutions. In the kitchen, for example, the floor surface and the benchtop extend from the interior to the outdoor courtyard. When the custom-made window is raised, it is transformed into an awning and the kitchen and courtyard form a single uninterrupted space. The architectural style of the extension is unashamedly contemporary, with expressed aluminium blade louvres and grilles introducing a raw industrial edge to the otherwise minimalist aesthetic.

Cottage Farm

Cowper Griffith Architects
Suffolk, UK

73

A traditional barn in the Suffolk countryside has been transformed by Cowper Griffith Architects into a contemporary home. Since the barn forms part of a cluster of farm buildings, the clients requested that exterior changes be kept to a minimum. In response, the architect created a series of external shutters for the doors and windows, which can be closed when the home is not in use, thereby returning the barn to its former appearance. Inside, the spaces are arranged around a curved wall that runs through the building, forming the entrance at one end and a balcony that projects over the pond at the other. This curvaceous aesthetic is mirrored in the spiralling form of the staircase and the bowed underside of the first floor, which creates unconventional ceilings below. Such quirky features as these ensure that, despite the change in use, this barn is brimming with character.

Baker Baxter House

Michael Drain

London, UK

74

Reached by a bridge across a stream, the Baker Baxter House in Barnes, west London, turns its back on passers-by, with only its wenge entrance doors facing the street. The walls, clad in a marble-aggregate-chip render, are crisp and slightly forbidding. Michael Drain was asked to create a discreet sanctuary where noise transfer from outside and between the rooms would be minimal. Natural light was vital, yet views out of the building had to be restricted to prevent the interiors being overlooked by neighbours. The result resembles a concrete bunker, with extensive glazing across the roof to provide natural light. A library runs through the centre of the house. From here, there is access to the entrance hall, the three bedrooms – each with en suite bathroom – and the open-plan dining and living area that occupies one side of the building. A study, a utility room and a kitchen are contained within concrete partitions. Custom-made storage units clad in white glass line many of the walls, while the floors are covered in a light grey limestone that continues to the two outdoor terraces.

252

G House

Jun Aoki & Associates
Tokyo, Japan

75

The most striking element of this Tokyo house – called 'G' by the architect – is the irregular form of its roof. The traditional pitch is shunted sideways to create a dramatic off-centre peak, which, together with its irregularly arranged windows, gives the building its unique and contemporary character. In fact, the whole house, which has a total area of 115 square metres (1670 sq. ft), is designed as a twist on convention. While the two upper storeys are timber-framed, a common practice in Japan, the ground floor and basement levels are cast out of solid concrete. The living-room, dining-room and kitchen are all in the concrete podium, while the bedrooms are in the upper section. The house is therefore split into two zones, with the divide expressed in the interior by a horizontal gap of 77.3 centimetres (2 ft 6 in.) between the top of the concrete plinth and the timber floor above. The lightness and flexibility of the timber frame enabled the inclusion of open-tread staircases and glass partition walls in the upper section of the building, allowing light to filter into the concrete-encased rooms below.

256

House VI

De Paor Architects

Dalkey, County Dublin, Ireland

76

Cut into a steep hillside in Dalkey, just south of Dublin, this spectacular two-storey family house, an angular building coated in a rich purple–grey acrylic render, makes a strong architectural statement while exploiting its panoramic views over the Irish Sea. Large plate-glass screens, set in specially made aluminium frames, cut through its solid form. The approach to the house provides tantalizing glimpses of the sea through the windows set on either side of the ground-floor living spaces, but not until the open-plan kitchen, living and dining area is the full magnificence of the outlook revealed. A triangular terrace extends the living area outdoors. On a lower level are the bedrooms, dug into the granite hillside, each carefully designed by the architects with a view through the surrounding trees to the sea. The bathrooms are arranged at the back of this lower level.

Farmhouse

77

McLean Quinlan
Totnes, Devon, UK

Tucked under the crest of a hill in rural Devon, not far from Totnes, this family home fits seamlessly into its surroundings, replacing an old farm that once stood on the site. When the original house was demolished, the client salvaged and cleaned all the old stones and used them to construct the walls of the new building. While reflecting local building traditions, the house was given a modern twist by the addition of large panes of glass inserted into the bulky stone walls; they provide magnificent views of the surrounding landscape. The interior spaces are arranged over three floors. The ground-floor spaces flow into one another, with the living, kitchen and dining areas all benefiting from sliding glass doors that open on to external terraces. The most impressive space is the master bedroom, which sits under the massive green-oak beams of the roof. While a large en suite bathroom is located at one end of the room, the other end is made entirely from glass, providing ever-changing views of the valley below.

Zinc House

HEAT Architecture
London, UK

78

At the core of this ultra-modern home in Islington, north London, is a brick house built in the 1950s for an officer at the nearby Pentonville prison. Subsequent owner and architect Charles Humphries, the director of HEAT Architecture, transformed the building after winning a two-year planning battle with the local council. First, Humphries opened up the ground-floor living space by adding a kitchen extension with a vaulted zinc roof and glass wall facing a small courtyard garden. Next, he removed the entire roof and front wall, creating a dramatic new street

façade in opaque glass and zinc. A third-storey master bedroom was added with a sliding glass wall leading to a south-facing balcony. The architect used the opportunity to improve the building's environmental performance. Existing cavity walls were stuffed with insulation and the extra storey was super-insulated. The water is partially heated by solar panels and a heat-recovery ventilation system runs through the building. It is a bold and sustainable project that shows how existing building stock can be improved to meet the demands of twenty-first-century living.

Waterside House

Allen Jack + Cottier

Sydney, New South Wales, Australia

79

This sprawling, luxurious home occupies a highly desirable position overlooking Vaucluse Bay in an eastern suburb of Sydney, Australia. Providing accommodation for a family of six, the two-storey waterside building was designed by Allen Jack + Cottier, with Tim Allison and Associates collaborating on the interior design. The house consists of a series of pavilions and courtyards leading off a central spine. The courtyards are arranged in such a way as to maximize the potential for combined indoor and outdoor living, while also offering the advantage of natural cross-ventilation and visually reducing the bulk of the building. At the heart of the home is the kitchen, which is connected to the informal dining area, living-room and extensive outdoor terrace. The rooms are somewhat decadently furnished, with limestone and polished timber flooring adorning the ground floor and detailed joinery conspicuous throughout. The predominant exterior material is glass, giving interesting views from almost every room of the boats bobbing in the bay.

80

Sylvanus House

Bere Architects

London, UK

This unashamedly modern house overlooks Highgate Cemetery, one of London's most historic and well-known burial grounds. The contrast between new and old is beguiling, especially at night, when the contemporary interiors can be seen from the outside illuminated through expansive areas of glass. Squeezed into a compact hillside site, the house consists of three storeys. The ground level accommodates the entrance hall and garage. Above this are the bedroom, a study and two bathrooms. The top floor is reserved for the kitchen, living and dining areas. It is this uppermost floor area that is the most impressive part of the house. Wrapped around two of its sides is a terrace that is connected to the interior spaces by floor-to-ceiling sliding glass doors. From here the owners can enjoy a panoramic view of the city. An overhanging roof canopy regulates summer heat gain. The angle of the roof adds interest to the pared-down rooms, while a woodburning stove provides a contemporary interpretation of the hearth at the centre of the home.

Coalpit House

Stiff + Trevillion

Haywards Heath, West Sussex, UK

81

A house was originally constructed on this sloping site near Haywards Heath in the 1970s. Built in a Scandinavian style using local bricks, the property was gradually extended over the years until the current owners commissioned the architect Stiff + Trevillion to remodel it radically. The new design strips away the recent additions and replaces them with glass-encased living spaces that wrap around the existing core. This allowed the architect to enlarge the ground-floor living spaces, insert an internal pool and reorganize circulation routes around the home with the inclusion of a double-height entrance hall. The sleeping accommodation was reorganized, a new garage added and the sloping garden extensively relandscaped. The three main living spaces and two master bedrooms are now ranged along the southern side of the building, with views to the distant South Downs.

276

Kamakura House

82

Foster + Partners

Kamakura, Kanagawa, Japan

Located in the coastal town of Kamakura, not far from Tokyo, this house was designed by the British architect Foster + Partners for a collector of Buddhist art. It forms part of a complex that includes an art gallery, a large reception space and a specialist storage unit. A Shinto shrine once stood on this site, and remains have been found of hand-dug caves that were part of an eleventh-century samurai-sword workshop. The overall composition of the buildings is intended to harmonize with the rugged landscape. A key element of the interiors is the subtle use of colour, with muted tones and dark ceilings creating an intimate and tranquil environment. Some specialist materials were developed for the project. For example, interior and exterior walls are clad in custom-made reconstructed stone, while glass blocks made from recycled television tubes provide diffused light. The floor surfaces are covered in part with antique Chinese tiles, and the indoor pool is finished in glazed volcanic rock. A sophisticated lighting system enhances the effect of these richly textured materials, while also illuminating the client's artworks.

Vaucluse House 1

JAHN Associates

Sydney, New South Wales, Australia

83

This four-bedroomed house is one of two properties built by JAHN Associates on a single plot overlooking the Vaucluse Bay area of Sydney Harbour (the other is no. 48). The building occupies a narrow, sloping piece of land shoehorned between a rocky hillside at the back and Kincoppal Convent at the front. The architect overcame these restraints by creating a compact house with tiered terraces that fully exploit the views across the water. The building is divided into three sections – bedrooms, living areas and circulation areas – each with a different

roof. Together with the interplay of rendered walls, large glazed areas, timber cladding and louvres, this gives the building a strong and distinctive aesthetic. Interior spaces are fairly small because of the narrowness of the site, but there are many windows and sliding glass doors that lead to balconies and terraces. At the base of the property is a swimming pool surrounded by a series of angular walls and steps. At night, one of these retaining walls glows orange, adding further dynamism to this cleverly designed home.

Broomfield Lane House

Plastik Architects
London, UK

84

The ground floor of this family house in the north London suburb of Palmers Green was remodelled by Plastik Architects to create a light-filled, open space specifically designed to meet the needs of its owners. The walls of the original property were demolished, reduced and re-sited to create a sleek fitted kitchen at the centre of the home. To one side is a dining-room defined by a specially made storage unit that serves both this room and the kitchen. On the other side, in what was formerly a garage, are a shower room and utility room. To the rear of the property, accessible directly from the kitchen, is a box-like garden room of timber and glass. Jutting 5 metres (16½ ft) into the garden, the garden room is defined on one side by a huge glass panel that wraps around part of the roof, and a sliding door flanked by floor-to-ceiling glass panes. This sliding door is designed as a piece of wall, with a square window inserted at its centre. Painted red on the inside, the door brings a playful touch to this cleverly reconstructed home.

286

House on Evening Hill

Horden Cherry Lee Architects

Poole Harbour, Dorset, UK

85

The prime objective for Horden Cherry Lee Architects when designing this family home was to achieve the best possible southward view over Poole Harbour. Glass and steel are therefore the predominant materials in the building, which covers 250 square metres (2690 sq. ft); all the major living areas and the four ground-floor bedrooms benefit from floor-to-ceiling, south-facing windows. The architect took advantage of the natural slope of the site by encasing the lower ground level in a concrete shell, which acts as a retaining structure and the foundation for the house above. The high thermal mass of the concrete helps to regulate the building's internal temperature. In winter, solar heat entering from the south is stored and gradually released by the concrete into the living spaces. In summer, the balcony overhang and adjustable scrim blinds prevent excessive solar heat gain. The house is cleverly designed as a series of 2.6-metre (8½-ft) structural bays, giving the clients the option to extend the house later by adding further bays to the western perimeter.

Summer House

Wingårdhs
Sweden

86

The design of this compact summer house was dictated by its remote position on Sweden's west coast, 30 kilometres (17 miles) north of Gothenburg. All building materials had to be shipped to the site and no equipment was available to blast foundations into the bedrock. The architect therefore decided on a lightweight timber structure on a timber deck. A steel frame was incorporated to support the double-height interior spaces. Planning rules limited the internal dimensions to 80 square metres (861 sq. ft), but floor space is maximized by the layout, which includes an open-plan kitchen, living and dining area, and three bedrooms, two located on mezzanine levels on either side of the double-height living zone. Large sliding doors in all the ground-floor rooms lead out to a timber deck. While the interior walls are painted a muted white, the exterior is clad in Canadian cedar with gutters made from open cedar planks. Left untreated, this cedar will turn a silvery grey, making it even more harmonious with the landscape that was so influential in the house's design.

Brick House

87

Caruso St John Architects
London, UK

The Brick House is shoe-horned into an awkward site between the backs of three Georgian terraces in Paddington, west London. From the street, the only hint of its existence is a ramp and a plain timber door, but the house occupies an area of 190 square metres (2045 sq. ft) and consists of a series of dramatic volumes. Virtually every surface is covered in honey-coloured Cambridge brick. The large open-plan kitchen, living and dining area on the first floor is topped with a cast-concrete ceiling 45 centimetres (18 in.) thick. The ceiling dips and rises in height to demarcate the various zones and is punctuated with triangular rooflights. A small study and bathroom are also on the first floor, while the ground floor is more intimate, with a narrow hallway leading to four bedrooms, two bathrooms and a utility room. Two courtyards and a garden reached from the bedrooms occupy the space between the building and the walls of the neighbouring houses. An unpromising scrap of land in the heart of the city has been transformed into a sculptural sanctuary.

Tamarama Houses

88

Jake Dowse Architects

Tamarama, New South Wales, Australia

These three connected houses are located in Tamarama, an eastern beachside suburb of Sydney, and perfectly reflect the informal spirit of the area. Built to replace two existing properties on the site, they make the most of the restricted space with a compact three-storey design. Simple in form, the white-painted houses are constructed from steel frames and concrete slabs, with rows of plantation blinds adding a decorative element. The interiors are bright and airy with free-flowing spaces, double-height atria and generous amounts of glass to allow

natural light to flood in. Folding glass doors at the rear of each home open on to rectangular gardens edged by a swimming pool that runs along the rear boundary of the site. The two bookend properties also incorporate outdoor kitchen areas, and roof terraces provide extra outside space to all three houses.

298

Butler's Wharf Apartment

89

Powell Tuck Associates
London, UK

This flat on the south bank of the River Thames is the product of a second collaboration between the clients and Powell Tuck Associates. The architect's first commission was to design a flat on the fourth floor of a riverside wharf in Shad Thames, a street near Tower Bridge. Having lived there for three years, the clients sold up and, to accommodate a growing family, bought a larger apartment two floors above their first. Powell Tuck was again commissioned to rearrange the internal layout to provide a luxurious living space with a contemporary aesthetic.

In response, the architect has created a series of flexible spaces that can be either opened up to one another or separated by means of solid but sleek timber doors. Decadent touches include an open-tread timber staircase that appears to hover elegantly above the floor, and a glass-enclosed gas fire located underneath the suspended television unit. A more informal atmosphere prevails in the combined kitchen and dining area, which includes a breakfast bar and a blackboard wall adorned with the ever-changing scribbles of the clients' children.

House on Musashino Hills

Waro Kishi and K. Associates/Architects

Tokyo, Japan

90

This house juts out dramatically from its hillside setting to take advantage of the view south over Tokyo's Tama River. Built on a 30-degree incline on three levels, the house appears to cascade down the slope. The uppermost floor, the only part of the house that is visible from the rear driveway, is a steel-and-glass box, which stands on a supporting concrete structure that encases the lower two floors. The client – a writer – works at home, and she briefed the architects to create a clear distinction in the internal layout between public and private rooms. The top floor, which provides magnificent views over the surrounding urban landscape, accommodates the living-room, kitchen and dining-room. The next level down is more private, with the bedroom and a large terrace. The lowest floor has its own entrance and accommodates the guest bedroom. While the top floor offers wonderful panoramas of the city, the lower levels are less exposed, with more intimate views of the surrounding trees.

Templewood

Enclosure Architects

London, UK

91

Enclosure Architects has ingeniously created this light and spacious apartment in the roofspace of an existing property in Hampstead, north London. By replacing the maze of original timber supports with a concealed steel skeleton, the architect succeeded in evoking a contemporary aesthetic while maximizing usable living space. The central living and dining area opens on to an exterior terrace through a large rectangular void fitted with folding glass doors. Leading off the main space are a galley kitchen, a bedroom and a bathroom.

The mezzanine level, reached by means of a staircase with delicate open treads, accommodates the study. Crisp and bright internal finishes are echoed in white-plastered walls and timber flooring, while diffuse illumination from sophisticated built-in light fittings softens the overall effect. The design engenders a feeling of weightlessness, sometimes giving the apartment's occupants the impression that they are floating among the surrounding trees.

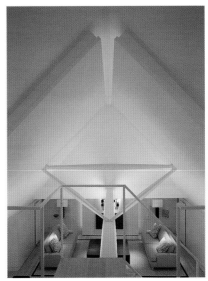

Richmond House

Brady Mallalieu Architects
Richmond, Surrey, UK

92

This contemporary home in Richmond, Surrey, was designed for a couple with three young children. The clients had previously lived in a traditional Victorian property and were keen to have more interconnected living spaces without resorting to an entirely open-plan layout. In response, the architect devised a groundbreaking plan that consists of rooms that can be opened or closed by a system of sliding doors and moving walls. The main living spaces are arranged in four towers, each 6 metres (20 ft) square, surrounding a central glass-roofed void. The floor levels in each tower are staggered, with short flights of stairs linking the various rooms. Seats, ledges and display recesses are built into the stair spaces. Ceiling heights vary from room to room, from a cosy study with low oak beams to a living-room 6 metres (20 ft) high. All the rooms either open on to or have internal windows looking on to the glass-roofed central space, an arrangement that allows daylight to penetrate the whole building. The kitchen has a dramatic glazed pyramid roof that admits yet more natural light.

Brae Street House

Chris Elliott Architects

Bronte, New South Wales, Australia

93

This house in Bronte, near Sydney, started life as one of a pair of single-storey, semi-detached cottages. In the 1960s one cottage was replaced by an ugly block of flats, which overlooked the rear garden of the other. The owners of the surviving cottage asked Chris Elliott Architects to find a solution that would both significantly enlarge their home and create a barrier between them and the flats. The result is a two-storey extension running from the back of the old house along the eastern boundary of the garden. The old house contains the original entrance hall, three bedrooms and a traditional lounge; the ground floor of the extension has a more informal, open-plan living, kitchen and dining area set on a concrete platform that juts out over the new swimming pool. While the lower level of the extension is lined with glass walls, the steel-clad upper level is more enclosed. It holds the master bedroom with an adjoining dressing-room and a bathroom built above a carport. A glass walkway leads from the bedroom suite to the attic of the old house, now converted into a work and play area.

Stealth House

Robert Dye Associates
London, UK

94

Stealth House stands between a Modernist detached house and an adjoining Edwardian terrace in south-east London. It replaces an ugly 1950s building, which was abruptly set back from the terrace. The new building, covering 200 square metres (2153 sq. ft), was designed by Robert Dye Associates with two different street-setback lines to reconcile it with its disparate neighbours. Of timber-frame construction, with stressed plywood panels to allow for the double cantilever at the corners, it is clad in black-stained Russian redwood. The house has an inner core, which is rendered in pale grey K-rend, a traditional Irish material made from crushed rubble. A gap separates the core from the redwood cladding, giving the impression that the outer skin is floating on the inner core. The roof, made from a grey–green mineralized felt, continues the line of the neighbouring brick house. From the street, Stealth House appears to be a two-storey black structure with a grey pitched roof, but the monopitch hides a third storey with a double bedroom and en suite bathroom opening on to a roof terrace, visible only from the rear.

Wetherby House

95

OMI Architects

Wetherby, West Yorkshire, UK

An elegant Georgian villa remodelled and updated by OMI Architects has been radically enhanced by the addition of a modern wing that respects the context of its older neighbour. The house is part of a row with gardens backing on to the River Wharfe in the centre of the West Yorkshire town of Wetherby. The setting had an important influence on the design of the extension, most of which is taken up by a new living-room. Large sliding glass doors make it possible to open up the room to a terraced area bounded by a glass balustrade. From here a series of tiered terraces leads down to the water's edge. Inside, traditional features, such as the original plaster ceiling moulds, combine successfully with clean-lined contemporary materials, including a latticed timber partition. Thoughtful in design and precisely executed, the harmonious extension has subtly breathed new life into an old home.

Courtyard Houses

Powell Tuck Associates
London, UK

96

On a site in west London previously occupied by a car workshop, Powell Tuck Associates has made two bright and spacious live/work units. Set behind a row of terraced houses, the properties are reached from the street by means of a subtly designed archway. The materials used are sympathetic to the surrounding brick houses but also reflect the site's industrial heritage. The external walls are clad in London stock brick and punctuated by sunscreens and cladding of western red cedar. The doors are made of Douglas fir, and the large panes of glass sit within aluminium frames. Since the site is shielded from the street and has a perimeter wall 4 metres (13 ft) high, the architect could include large amounts of glass on the ground floor without diminishing the occupants' privacy. The interiors are given a utilitarian feel by the use of such rough, inexpensive finishes as exposed-brick and breezeblock walls and steel-tread staircases, materials that complement the crisp lines of the building. Some of the glass screens can be opened to give access to small back gardens.

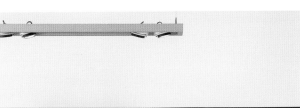

O House

Sou Fujimoto Architects
Chiba, Japan

97

The owners of this house overlooking a rocky stretch of the Japanese coast, two hours' drive from Tokyo, asked Sou Fujimoto Architects to create a building that fully exploited its closeness to the Pacific Ocean. In response, the architect came up with a concrete-encased structure that consisted of a single open-plan space with branch-like wings stretching away from the central fulcrum. A person moving through any one of these wings will enjoy constantly changing views across the ocean through the extensively glazed walls. The architect likens this experience to walking along a coastal footpath: while some areas of the home offer wide panoramas, others allow mere glimpses of the water through narrow slits of glass. Comfortable spaces in which to relax and take in the sights are scattered along the trail. This is an original and clever design, beautifully executed. The exposed concrete walls of the interior, for example, bear the tactile marks of the shutters in which they were cast. The simplicity of the furnishings ensures that the sea views dominate throughout.

Hampstead House

Found Associates

London, UK

98

Found Associates granted a new lease of life to this large family home in Hampstead, north London, by extensively remodelling its interiors. On the ground floor, grey stone floors were laid throughout to give the property a unified and contemporary feel. At the centre of the home is the new kitchen, designed around a central white Corian block incorporating the hob, a range of appliances and a breakfast bar. The connecting dining area incorporates french windows that open to an outdoor terrace overlooking the swimming pool. From here the owners can see the new oak-clad pool house – also designed by Found Associates – at the far end of the garden. The bedrooms and bathrooms on the first floor of the main house were also remodelled in a clean-lined, modern style. Within the master suite, for example, a cantilevered walnut unit wraps around a wall to provide capacious storage for the dressing-room. The combination of luxurious materials with careful attention to detail does much to ensure the success of this project.

Provence House

99

KallosTurin

Cap d'Antibes, Alpes-Maritimes, France

Created by the international design company KallosTurin, this house in Provence exudes a sense of calm. It is located outside a medieval hilltop town overlooking Cap d'Antibes. The building that originally occupied the site was completely stripped back, both externally and internally, to create a minimalist home, with generous open-plan living spaces devoid of clutter and superfluous details. The palette of materials is very simple, with muted colour tones specially selected to accentuate the warmth of the light in this part of France. While the walls are painted white, a pale amber limestone is featured in floors, stairs, walls, counters and benches, providing visual connections between the various rooms. The limestone is also used in the exterior terrace, drawing the eye out of the house towards an infinity-edge lap pool and the magnificent view beyond.

340

100 HOUSES

Murray Mews

ACQ

London, UK

This modern mews house in Camden, north London, is the brainchild of ACQ (now part of FLACQ). In contrast with traditional mews houses, which frequently provide dark and impractical living accommodation, this home is filled with natural daylight and provides flexible bedrooms and areas for play and study. The unusual layout includes a double-height kitchen, living and dining space overlooked by a play deck. This arrangement of rooms, coupled with generous expanses of glass, allows natural light to filter through to the core of the building. The bedrooms are private and enclosed spaces, but the uppermost floor comprises a work studio with access to a terrace at both the front and the rear. These roof decks and the small rear garden, reached through sliding floor-to-ceiling glass doors, make it possible for family life to be carried on outdoors as well as indoors. From the exterior, the form of the building may look straightforward, but the meticulously thought-out arrangement of rooms inside conveys an impression of spaciousness on a restricted site.

Photography Credits

All photographs are supplied by VIEW and are copyright © the individual
photographers, as listed below.

l = left, r = right, t = top, b = bottom

1 Dennis Gilbert
2 Peter Cook
3 Richard Glover
4 Edmund Sumner
5 Edmund Sumner
6 Edmund Sumner
7 Edmund Sumner
8 Richard Glover
9 Edmund Sumner
10 Peter Cook
11 Edmund Sumner
12 James Brittain
13 Philip Bier
14 Nick Guttridge
15 Kilian O'Sullivan
16 Dennis Gilbert
17 Richard Glover
18 Chris Gascoigne
19 Christian Michel
20 Dennis Gilbert
21 Chris Gascoigne (pages 77tl, 78l,
tr, 79tr, bl, br); Dennis Gilbert
(pages 76, 77tr, b, 78br, 79tl)
22 Edmund Sumner
23 Hufton + Crow
24 Edmund Sumner

25 Richard Glover
26 Allan Crow
27 Peter Cook
28 Richard Glover
29 Peter Cook
30 Richard Glover
31 Dennis Gilbert
32 Raf Makda
33 Peter Cook
34 Dennis Gilbert
35 Dennis Gilbert
36 Edmund Sumner
37 Robert Such
38 Philip Bier
39 Edmund Sumner
40 Edmund Sumner
41 Peter Cook
42 Chris Gascoigne
43 Richard Glover
44 Peter Cook
45 Hufton + Crow
46 Peter Cook
47 Dennis Gilbert
48 Richard Glover
49 Nick Hufton
50 Hufton + Crow

51 Dennis Gilbert
52 Peter Cook
53 Dennis Gilbert
54 Hufton + Crow
55 Peter Cook
56 Julie Phipps
57 Edmund Sumner
58 Peter Cook
59 Raf Makda
60 Philip Bier
61 Sue Barr
62 Edmund Sumner
63 Dennis Gilbert
64 Richard Glover
65 Hufton + Crow
66 Edmund Sumner
67 Richard Glover
68 Hufton + Crow
69 Edmund Sumner
70 Dennis Gilbert
71 Dennis Gilbert
72 Richard Glover
73 Peter Cook
74 Dennis Gilbert
75 Edmund Sumner
76 Dennis Gilbert

77 Peter Cook
78 Kilian O'Sullivan
79 Richard Glover
80 Peter Cook
81 Dennis Gilbert
82 Edmund Sumner
83 Richard Glover
84 Edmund Sumner
85 Dennis Gilbert
86 Robert Such
87 Ioana Marinescu
88 Richard Glover
89 Edmund Sumner
90 Edmund Sumner
91 Paul Tyagi
92 Dennis Gilbert
93 Richard Glover
94 Andy Stagg
95 Dennis Gilbert
96 Edmund Sumner
97 Edmund Sumner
98 Hufton + Crow
99 Dennis Gilbert
100 Hufton + Crow

Index

The website address for each
architect is given below. Details
were correct at the time of printing.

Author's acknowledgements

I should like to thank the Merrell team, in particular Julian Honer for commissioning this book, and Nicola Bailey, who oversaw its design. A special thank you goes to Rosanna Fairhead, who has, as always, been an absolute pleasure to work with, and who has shown great commitment and skill in project-managing this book.

I should also like to thank VIEW – particularly Yvonne Peeke-Vout, Sophia Gibb and all the photographers – for all the wonderful images, and the architects whose projects have made 100 Houses possible. Finally, I should like to thank my family for their constant and unwavering support.

First published 2009 by Merrell Publishers Limited

81 Southwark Street
London SE1 0HX

merrellpublishers.com

British Library Cataloguing-in-Publication data:
Strongman, Cathy
100 houses : modern designs for contemporary living
1. Architecture, Domestic 2. Architecture, Modern – 21st century
3. Interior decoration
I. Title II. One hundred houses III. A hundred houses
728.3'7'09051

ISBN 978-1-8589-4469-2

Produced by Merrell Publishers Limited
Designed by Grade Design Consultants, London
Copy-edited by Henrietta Heald
Proof-read by Sarah Yates

Printed and bound in China

Jacket front: Szirtes House by Chenchow Little Architects (no. 64)
Jacket back: Holly Barn by Knox Bhavan Architects (no. 35)
Page 2: Esher House by Wilkinson King Architects (no. 38)
Page 4: Portobello Road Houses by Alan Power Architects (no. 68)
Pages 12–13: Butterfly House by Chetwoods Architects (no. 9)